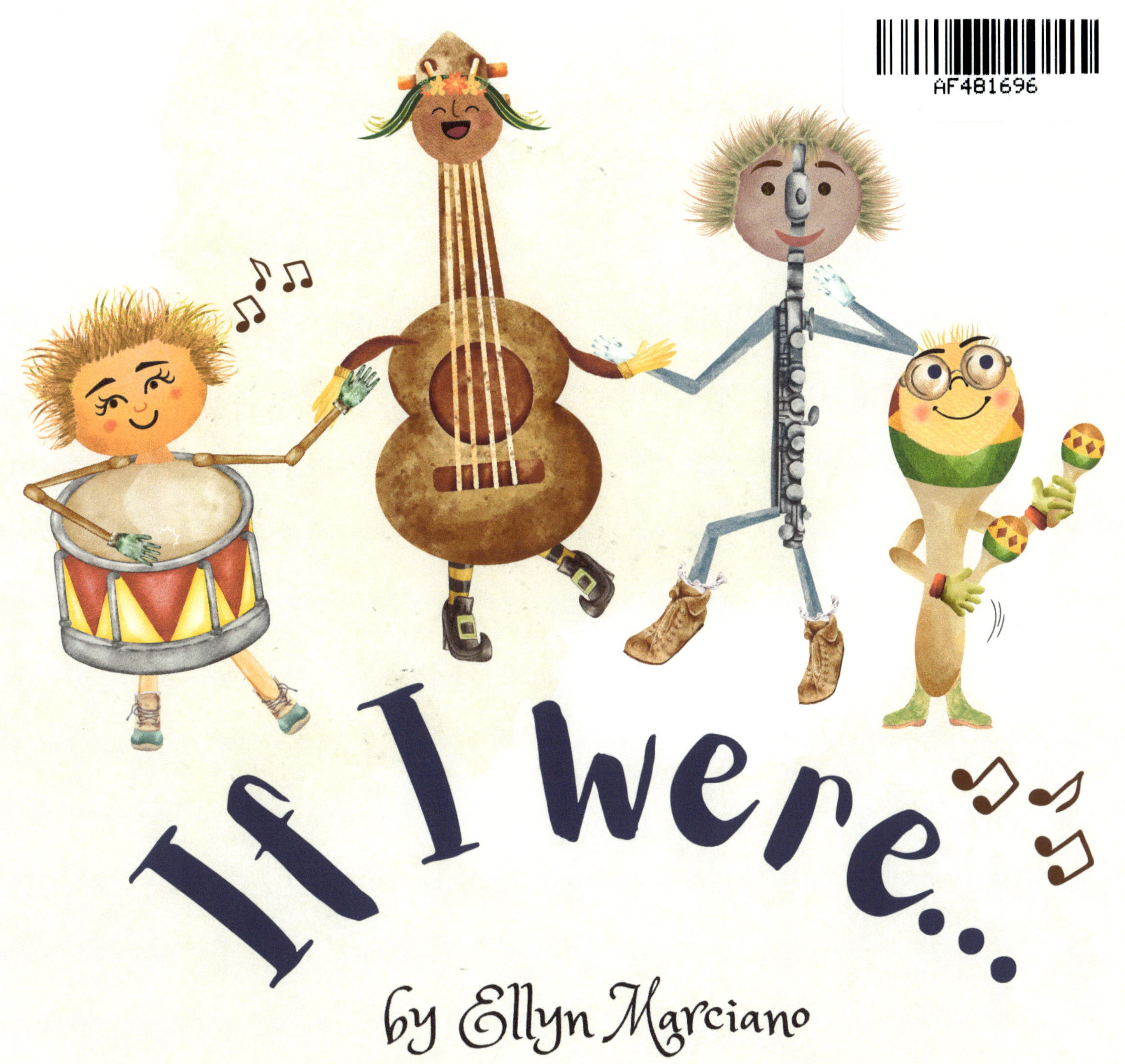

If I were...

by Ellyn Marciano

This book belongs to

____

If I were a drum, I'd
BOOM! BOOM!
BOOM!

Marching all around my

ROOM ROOM
ROOM
ROOM

If I were a drum, I'd
BOOM!
BOOM! BOOM!
BOOM!

And that's how I'd say,

"Hello"!

If I were a GUITAR, I'd

STRUM STRUM
STRUM

Dancing while I sing and

HUM HUM HUM

If I were a GUITAR, I'd
STRUM STRUM
STRUM

And that's how I'd say,
"Hello"!

If I were a MARACA, I'd
SHAKE
SHAKE
SHAKE

Such a happy noise, I'd

MAKE MAKE

MAKE

If I were a MARACA, I'd

And that's how I'd say,

"Hello"!

If I were a flute, I'd

TOOT TOOT TOOT TOOT

Singing in my shiny
SUIT
SUIT SUIT
SUIT

If I were a flute, I'd
TOOT
TOOT
TOOT
TOOT

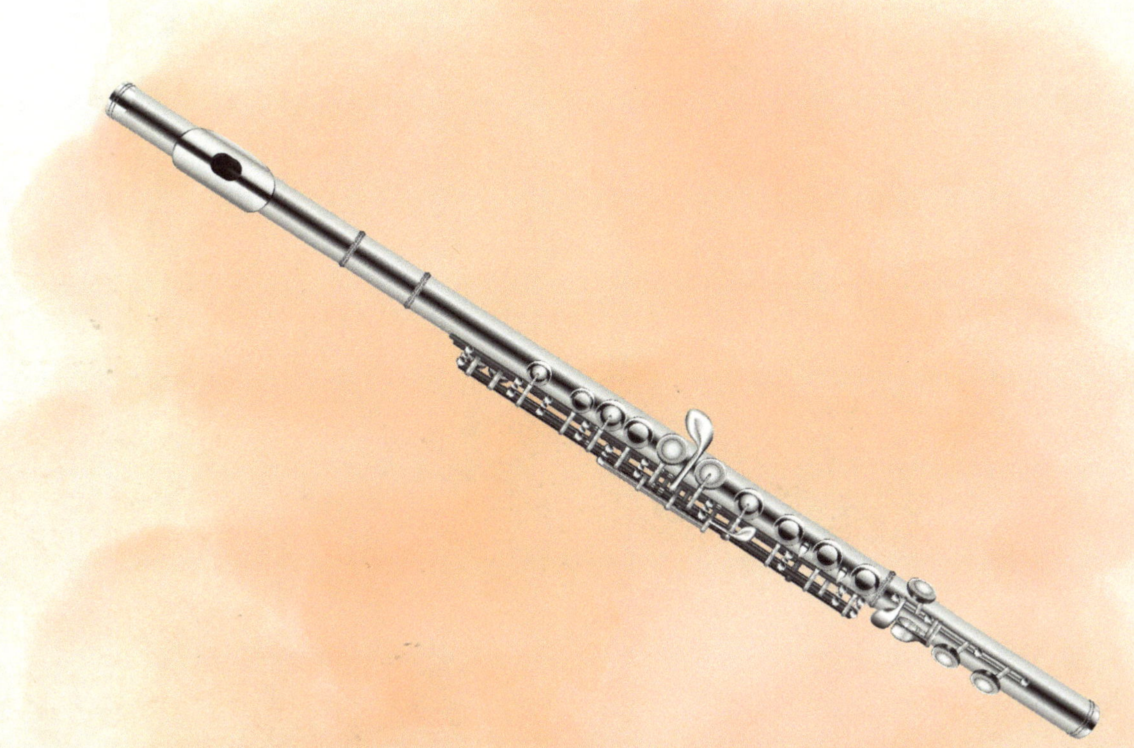

And that's how I'd say,

"Hello"!

BOOM, BOOM!
STRUM, STRUM!

SHAKE, SHAKE!
TOOT, TOOT!

That's how we say

HELLO!

**Listen to "If I Were...";
an original song by
Ellyn Marciano.**

© 1988; Ellyn Marciano - Ellyn's Songs for Young Children